ATTICUTION

WHY SUCCESS EQUALS
ATTITUDE PLUS EXECUTION

ELTON HART

HIGH BRIDGE BOOKS
HOUSTON

Contents

Introduction

Atticution: noun
> carrying out or putting into motion a
> plan or course of action with a
> positive mental attitude

Atticute: verb
> carry out a plan fully with a positive
> mental attitude

What is atticution? Atticution is the ability to execute a given task while maintaining a positive mental attitude. If you're going to do anything worthwhile, you will be met with some level of resistance. The bigger your goal or higher your ambition, the larger the obstacles, the bigger the resistance, and the more vocal people will be on how you can't do it. You must push through the short pain or discomfort, refuse to listen to those around you, maintain your positive attitude, and execute on the small daily/weekly tasks that will lead to successfully accomplish your goals.

Why am I writing this book?

I have seen too many of my personal friends and professional cohorts fail to reach their full potential because they either lack the right attitude when times get hard or lack the execution needed to deliver results. "Attitude + execution = success" resonates from the entry-level students I taught in Krav Maga self-defense classes to the top-level executives I work with every day. As I mentor more and more people at all levels, the constant theme is that either the wrong attitude or lack of execution keeps them from reaching the next level. The need for this book became very clear to me when I realized that one-on-one coaching would not reach my personal goal of the number of people I wanted to help.

My hope is that this book will serve as a catalyst for you and your personal growth and will positively impact those you love. From setting SMAART goals (yes, that is an extra "A"—more details in chapter five) to building a strong accountability tribe, you own your growth. You will need to lean in and take the time to reflect at the end of each chapter, complete the work-sheets, and execute the tasks given throughout the book. The more effort you put into this book, the more you will get out of it, or in *Atticution* terms, the more you execute with the right atti-tude, the more rewarding your results will be.

Let's face it: we have all been there. You or someone you know had an excellent idea, maybe even the proverbial "Million Dollar Idea," only to see someone somewhere else a year later sell-ing that idea on TV or online and making a mint. The only thing different was they *executed*. They had the same idea and the right positive attitude when those around them said, "Yeah, it's a good idea, but…" then listed ten reasons why it would fail. But they had the *Atticution* spirit and deliv-ered on their dreams and their goals.

To get the most out of this book…

To get the most out of this book, read through it entirely, then come back and read each chapter, really diving into the questions at the end. The more you lean into the questions, the more you will get out of the book. Each chapter has a rele-vant story and detailed chapter content, ending with an *Attitude Check* and an *Execution Exercise*.

This is designed to challenge you to execute immediately and start your momentum and behavior-building habits. Once you begin to atticute daily, you will see a positive shift in your life and a positive impact on those around you.

As you begin to atticute your goals and personal development, you will quickly find that you will have to adjust and reset your goals since *you will* meet or exceed your original targets. This book will serve as a resource when you need to adjust your targets, and the *Attitude* and *Execution* exercises' answers will look different each time you answer them. Keep your original answers as they are a great reflection document as you set bigger and more aggressive targets and goals.

Now let's atticute!

—Elton Hart
President
Atticution Training, Inc.
1410 Magnolia Park Circle
Cumming, Ga 30040
www.atticution.com

1

Motivation Is Just an Alarm Clock

The starting point of all achievement is desire.

—Napoleon Hill

Motivation is everywhere. Tv commercials, songs, sports teams, magazines, and, of course, social media are littered with motivational memes, quotes, stories, etc. YouTube has countless hours of motivational videos, from three-minute clips to hour-long videos. I often use social media's powerful content to spark my motivation, but then I have to take action, or I will not gain any momentum.

Motivation is just an alarm clock; what gets results is what you do after you get "motivated." This is seen every January as most of the world sets—or at least thinks about setting—New Year's resolutions. As a life-long gym guy, I see this play out every year. I used to be bothered by all the new people taking up cardio equipment, leaving plates and dumbbells everywhere, or just sitting on machines glued to their phones, among other instances of annoying gym etiquette. Now, I am happy to see people getting started and am glad they didn't put it off more by hitting the snooze and telling themselves that same old "I'll-start-next-Monday" excuse. I even go out of my way to help, if possible, engaging them and trying to be a welcoming person. I know that the gym can be and usually is an intimidating environment, so the fact that they have taken the first and most difficult step is fantastic.

We have this saying in field sales: "The hardest door to open is the car door." What we mean is that you must get in the field and get out of your comfy car in front of customers to make sales. Getting out of your head and knocking on the door is the only way to make progress. Just like all those highly motivated people who signed up for the gym, purchased great new gym outfits, laid out their clothes for the next day, and threw out all the snacks in the house, now it's time to execute.

In the beginning, finding a daily motivation alarm clock was key for me, and I found mine with my phone. I was starting back to school to get my MBA at the University of Georgia, traveling 20+ days a month for work, and had just moved my family to northern Georgia. Additionally, my boys were starting new schools, and I still wanted to work out regularly, so I needed more time. As we all know, a day's length doesn't change, so I needed to get up earlier to get more out of every single day.

I used my phone as my early morning alarm clock (like 4:30 a.m. early) but changed the sound from that same old alarm clock sound to the sound of Dr. Eric Thomas, "the hip-hop preacher," giving one of his highly motivational talks. Now, if you've never heard Dr. Thomas give a motivational speech, you need to jump on YouTube and search for him. Imagine getting woken up every day with a motivational speech! I would hear Dr. Thomas's voice as I woke from my slumber, and my brain would automatically start running and remind me why I set that alarm so early, why I must get up, and why I must attack the day. Even if I'd had a long day before with a body-draining workout and a delayed flight that got me into my hotel closer to 1 a.m. than 9 p.m., I knew it was time, and I had to move and execute. Getting up and moving starts the momentum of the day and leads to daily progress toward your goals. Once this became a habit, I would exchange my daily alarms with other songs and speakers, often aligning my current goals with the alarm sounds/songs.

This daily routine to start my day was a great catalyst for me and a constant reminder that this was not a one-time thing. I had set extremely high goals, and only daily execution would deliver the extraordinary results I was expecting. This daily routine is just one example of a small but meaningful "alarm clock" I set up to drive me. You will have to find your own motivational alarm clock. Ensure that it is not just an alarm clock but a force that will pull you toward your goals.

Attitude Check

- When was the last time you felt motivated?

- What actions did you take or not take to act in that moment?

- What can you use as a daily alarm clock to get you motivated?

Execution Exercise

- List your top three motivation sources, such as family, friends, videos, etc.

- List two or more people who can help you stay motivated.

- Find an event with a defined date to focus on (e.g., 5k fun run, half marathon, vacation, wedding, re-union, etc.), anything that can help push you toward your goal. *And* sign up today to do it! Take action *now*! Seriously—stop, find it, and sign up!

  o Communicate your event and the date to those you trust and can help hold you accountable.

2

Accountability Partners: Build Your Tribe

Surround yourself with people who force you to level up.

—Anonymous

As a very good friend delivered his top five annual goals to the accountability group, he was stopped in his tracks when we asked the third "why" question. He thought about it, and when he said, "I just don't think I'm good enough for her," we all had very surprised looks on our faces. We had known him and his wife for years, and on top of that, he was a tough East Coast guy who never really shared feelings. He continued and was extremely open. He explained his why, how he thought and his action (or lack thereof) lead him to this conclusion. We gave counsel, provided our perspective, and asked even more questions as he began to build his goals to strengthen his family and purposefully improve his relationship with his wife. I asked a simple question: "Have you ever said this to her?" He replied that he had not. We all agreed that just starting the conversation with her would go a long way toward a more purposeful relationship with her.

Before we let him move on to his next goal, I pushed just a little more. "So when will you have this conversation?" I asked.

He said, "Next week."

"What day next week?"

He said, "We usually have the most free time on Sunday."

"What time on Sunday?"

"Around two."

I asked, "Around two or at two? One last question: how will you ensure you don't have distractions and that you can focus on her, her response, the unforeseen response she might have, etc.?"

He grew quiet and thoughtful. We were all sales guys in the accountability group, so we knew the drill: *ask a question and shut up*. He finally said, "I will schedule a sitter for the kids and remove a level of distractions. I'll make reservations at a local restaurant, so I have to meet at a set time to limit even more distractions." He did have the conversation, and it turned out to be a great growth moment for him and his family. As the first person to review their goals with the group, this really set the tone for the rest of us and the offsite retreat.

This story is one of many examples of when we would gather and present our goals, both long term and short term. We now meet once a year to review and present our goals, discussing in great detail our "why" for each of those goals. We push each other to the point of discomfort from a place of love. The power of this group is that we have known each other for years and have a solid foundation of trust that allows us to call each other out if needed or just push each other to an uncomfortable place to help drive growth.

Building your tribe must be one of (if not *the*) top priority. The number one reason we fail at hitting our goals or even completing a task is that we lack accountability. Have you ever been two weeks into your "new" workout/diet plan but gotten hungry late at night and found yourself standing in front of the refrigerator looking for that zero-calorie snack that tastes delicious?

Without any accountability, it is easy to just eat that snack, just go to the gym tomorrow, just stop drinking next weekend, or just start on Monday, and the list goes on and on.

This is no different for your personal development. Without someone to assist in some level of accountability, slipping is easy. Progress, not perfection, is the goal, and when you know you have someone who cares about you and is willing to hold you accountable from a place of love, it makes the task/action much easier to accomplish. This can be a single person or a small group. I would not exceed five in a group; the more people you have, the more personality challenges you will encounter. I have found that, even with a small group, some will fall out because it is still work; when you're not moving forward, it is hard for some to continue. This is okay because it allows you to build stronger bonds with the ones dedicated to helping you be the best you.

I would suggest that you meet at a neutral location with minimal distractions. For our first session, we met at a beach house at least a few hours away from each of us. We brought our food and beverages so we could have organic conversations along with planned discussions.

We all had pre-work. I sent some loose guidelines on pre-work expectations, such as bringing a list of top five long-term goals, 20 other goals, and next year's annual to give us a starting place. We meet in mid-November since I like to have my annual goals fully locked in by late November. I start working on them before Thanksgiving, giving me a 20% head start on the year.

Everyone should be prepared to discuss in great detail their goals and their *why*. The group has the responsibility of asking the hard questions, and as my good friend, Felipe, would say, there is "no pretty talk," only real and meaningful conversations taking place. Each person must walk away with their very detailed and updated goals and their clearly defined next steps. The group also outlines their next steps, including when we will check in, when we will meet again, and how we will hold each other accountable.

Side note: as the unofficial leader of this group, I have found that proactively sending monthly updates via email are a fantastic accountability tool and drive me to exceed my goals—every single one!

Just start! You can try to plan the perfect location and date, but surprise—there isn't one. So just start!

Where do you start? When do you meet? With which topics should you start? What are the next steps?

Attitude Check

- Who in your circle of influence (professional and personal) can you trust and ask for help?

- In what areas of your life would you like some accountability?

- When could you meet, and how often?

Execution Exercise

- Make a list of five people you trust and value who can keep you accountable.

- Schedule a call with your list and explain your *why* and how you value them. Then tell them you would appreciate their help.

- Schedule a specific time at a distraction-free location with these five to communicate your goals

and let them know how they can
help you and vice versa.

For more information about workshops, setting
up your own offsite retreat, or facilitating a
workshop for you and your accountability
group, go to www.atticution.com.

3

Challenge Yourself

*Only those who dare to fail greatly can
ever achieve greatly.*

—Robert F. Kennedy

Even the best need to be challenged. Early in my career
with a major telco company, I was asked to take
my outside sales leadership skills and lead an already high performing inside sales team. I had
never even taken an inbound sales call, let alone
led an inside sales team. But I was up for the challenge and was excited to work with this highly
accomplished team. After spending the first 90
days observing, taking calls, learning the numbers, and building relationships, I posted our
new team goals. I not only communicated the aggressive goals with the team, but I also made it

publicly known that we would reach these new, never-before-reached goals in 60 days. Along with posting the new aggressive numbers on my office wall, I emailed the entire team and copied many leaders up the chain of command. Bold? Definitely! Brash? Maybe! But I saw the potential this team had; they just needed a challenge and a reward.

Within hours of receiving the email, the top inside sales rep for the entire region burst into my office, sat down, and let me know her thoughts. She was not afraid of sharing her opinion, and as the team's voice at the time, she had significant influence with the team. I knew if she got on board, we would crush the new goals. Sher started by saying, "I liked the old boss; he is a good guy and great leader. You might know how things work in the field, but it's different here. I know the company you came from and the people you worked with, and I don't care for them." She then pointed to the wall and said, "We can't do those numbers."

I listened, truly seeking to understand, and I said, "Okay, why not?"

"We have never done them, call volume is down, and we are understaffed."

"Understood. So if we get call volume up and get to full staff, can we do it?"

"We would need one heck of a lift in call volume and the right people, not just anyone." She not only knew her number, but she knew all the numbers.

"What percentage of call lift do we need? What does the right person look like?"

She explained what lift we needed and what the best people looked like. Once she finished, I asked, "So if we get the call lift and people hired, it's possible?"

"We've never seen volume that high."

"That's not what I asked. I asked if it's possible."

She said, "Yes, it's possible."

"Good, then we can do it."

She just looked at me and said again, "We can't hit those numbers," and left the office.

What I knew was that a focused team could accomplish almost any task given. The number became our rally cry, and we drove to the numbers. When leadership talked to the team, they spoke about the goal and the progress we were making toward the numbers. We had a goal, and we had a challenge. Was it a stretch? Yes! Was it going to take some sweat equity? Yes! Was it possible? *Yes!*

I am not an office guy, so I had facilities get me a small rolling table and a rolling chair. I built what I called an MCC (Mobile Command Center) with my laptop and wireless phone, which allowed me to work side by side with every rep and listen to sales interactions, even while checking emails. I was able to coach on the fly and lead from the front, even taking calls with reps as needed. The MCC was and still is one of my favorite sales activities in my entire career. My favorite was when senior leadership would be looking for me and find me wheeling my mobile command from sales cube to sales cube—the looks on their faces were priceless.

The approach of challenging and leading from the front started to pay off quickly. In the first full month with the new goals, we missed the mark by 15% but had the biggest sales month ever. In month number two, we hit our goal, and we hit it with a full selling day to spare! Bright and early on the first day of the new month, as I was prepping the new goals in my office, the sales rep burst in again.

"We did it! We hit the numbers."

"I know, with a full day to spare." Then I added, "Now we have to increase that by 10%."

She started to say, "We ca…" She stopped herself, and when I looked up, she smiled and said, "We can totally hit that!"

We have heard over and over that we should write down our goals and visit them often. I am shocked by the number of people I talk to who not only have not written their goals down but also cannot list at least five things they want to accomplish this year. It's been written that 3% of people write their goals down and 10% have goals in their minds, so that leaves 87% of people with no goals! This statistic holds true with the people I speak with across the country. So we know that we need to do it, but we don't. *Execution*! I have spent the last few months speaking with top salespeople in my industry, and these numbers hold true among the top 10% of sales producers. Imagine what could happen if they wrote down their goals? We will dive deeper into SMAART goals later in the book.

Challenging yourself is not easy and can even be very uncomfortable, but it is required for growth.

Attitude Check

- What new skill or challenge have you completed in the last 90 days?

- What new books have you read or classes have you taken in the last year?

- What is your limiting factor for why you're not challenging yourself?

Execution Exercise

- *Go write your goals down! Now.* Seriously, jump to the appendix of this book and write them down.

    o Your goals need to stretch you.

    o Communicate your goals with friends and family. I have found that telling my boys is the ultimate accountably.

4

Write It Down: Goals, Action Items, Commitments

A goal is a dream with a deadline.

—Napoleon Hill

After a few hours of conversation around sales numbers, headcount issues, training concerns, and leadership turnover, I asked the seasoned field director, "What are your top five goals for your team and yourself?" He stopped and looked at me with the look I see over and over again—*what does this have to do with my sales numbers?* So I clarified, "I know you have sales numbers to hit; we all do. And we all have the same human resources struggles, but all of this is a reflection of the leadership you as a director set. So again, I ask, what are your top five goals for your team and your-self?"

The director stopped and laughed a little (a nervous, uncomfortable laugh), then started to rattle off sales goals, forecast numbers, and other corporate data points.

"Stop right there! All of that is the result of your activity—what are the overall goals of your 70-plus-person sales team? Where are you going? Why are you going there, and why should your team care?"

He paused again, then said, "To be the number one sales team in the division, to hit 400 data sales [an all-time high for the market, not just his team], to be the cradle of leadership development for the division, to create a world-class sales organization."

"Solid start," I commented, "but where is that written down? How does your team know that?"

After a long pause and a moment of clarity, he pointed to his heart and said, "They've got it here."

Without skipping a beat, I asked again, "How do they know that?"

This is not an isolated incident. I have asked this same question to every leader I spend time with. The answer, 99% of the time, is their monthly/annual quota or forecast. So I clarify, "Okay, besides the goals that someone else has set for you, what are *your* top five goals, both professional and personal?" That's when I get looks that communicate thoughts like these: *I have never stopped and thought about it; crap, I don't have any;* and *I don't need this—I have them all in my head.*

So I ask, "Okay, where are they written down?"

"Well, uh, uh, well, I know them."

Great, but who else knows them? Did you hire all clairvoyant staff so they know what you're thinking? The truth is that 99% of the leaders I have worked with have little to no clear goals for themselves or their team. It's our job as leaders to set the pace and the tone for our teams. Setting goals is paramount to success.

Attitude Check

- What is your attitude toward goals?

- What is stopping you from writing your goals down?

Execution Exercise

- What are your top five goals in these categories?
  - ○ Professional
  - ○ Health: Fitness, Emotional, Spiritual, and Social
  - ○ Financial
  - ○ Personal Development
- Review these goals with your accountability partner or tribe, a trusted friend, a co-worker, or someone else.
- If you are a leader, schedule time with your team and build your top five team goals together.
  - ○ If you're not a leader yet, this will go a long way with your leadership since they might not have had the chance to do this themselves.
  - ○ *Side note*: setting team goals as a single unit builds unity and trust.

- Communicate with as many people as possible; this will help hold you accountable.

5

SMAART Goals

Goals are the fuel in the furnace of achievement.

—Brian Tracy

Only five months into my journey with my accountability group, I was drafting that month's email to the team. We had agreed that we would send out monthly updates to the entire group of our goals and our overall progress toward each goal as a way to hold each other accountable. I was very pleased with my update because I had made major progress in all but one area of my goals. I had even fully accomplished one of them, so I was more than happy to share with the team. Only two other group members had replied with their goals, so I pressed the group since we had agreed that we could challenge each other to ensure we were truly holding each other accountable. This continued for a few more months. We would move into a new month, and I would be the first to send updates to the group. Each month all but one other person would either say, "Nothing new to report," or would send very little information. Now, mind you, I gave a detailed update for every goal—even ones that didn't show progress.

It took only ten months for me to complete two major life goals. Only ten months from setting them and writing them down to hitting them—so I set new bigger goals. As I sat down to reflect and send my monthly update to my accountability tribe, I asked myself, *Why am I hitting my goals faster than my peers? Why do my updates seem to report more progress made or even include things that I've fully accomplished?* Then it hit me like a *lightning bolt:* I was not only revisiting my goals and emailing a progress report to my tribe every month, but I was also holding myself accountable for my success. All of the goals were specific, measurable, actionable, realistic, and timebound, but only mine had the missing ingredient: accountability.

We have all heard you need to make SMART goals, which are Specific, Measurable, Actionable or Attainable, Realistic, and Timebound. These are all true and are all great places to start since 87% of people don't even have goals, and only 3% actually write them down. I have always felt that something was missing in this model, and on that day, as I reflected on my goals, I realized what was missing—accountability!

The missing piece is holding yourself accountable to the goal. Who can help hold you accountable to your personal goals, and how can you hold yourself accountable? With our professional goals, we all have a boss, customers, or a team that holds us accountable to our daily, weekly, monthly, and annual goals. In our personal lives, we have very little, if any, accountability. We set personal goals all the time, but with no accountability, we either slowly slip or completely stop chasing the thing we wanted so badly.

This statement is never truer than with fitness and health. I love being in shape, but getting there takes discipline and focus. As a competitive bodybuilder and powerlifter, I have learned that 90% of any healthy program is diet, but we are the only ones who control what we consume. It is said (and is very true) that "you cannot out-train a bad diet." Sorry, but it's true; trust me, I've tried. So if diet is the biggest driver in a healthy body, it's easy to see why so many people struggle with reaching their fitness and health goals. We are all moving at lightning speed and grabbing whatever we can find before becoming *hangry* is a real struggle. You have to find ways to hold yourself accountable to the fitness goal you set.

Whether it's a fitness goal or a personal development goal, you must add accountability to your goal setting, or you will continue to struggle with accomplishment.

Attitude Check

- When was the last time you were able to reach a goal you set?

- What goals would bring you the most joy if you reached them in the next 12-24 months?

- What are the major obstacles that you would face in reaching those goals?

Execution Exercise

- Write down at least 20 goals leveraging the SMAART system (use the worksheet on the following page).

  o Goal: Define your goal with all the SMAART goal criteria and be as detailed as possible.

  o Term: Identify whether this is a short-term, medium-term, or long-term goal.

  o Accountability: Define how or by whom you will be held accountable to this goal.

  o Success: What does success look like?

SMAART Work Sheet

Goal	Term	Accountability	Success
1.			
2.			
3.			
4.			
5.			
6.			
7.			
8.			
9.			
10.			
11.			
12.			
13.			
14.			
15.			
16.			
17.			

SMAART Goals

18.			
19.			
20.			

6

Do What Winners Do — Grind

We are what we repeatedly do.
Excellence, then, is not an act, but a
habit.

—Aristotle

Very early in my retail sales career, I learned that winners *grind* ... which reminds me of my very first big sales contest! The prize was an all-expenses-paid trip to the Caribbean. As a young, single, cash-strapped man, I was more than thrilled to win this contest. I was in my first true sales job out of the Navy and was still learning the sales process and what did and didn't work. The contest was a simple point-based program: ten points for new sales, two points for accessories, and one point for payments. The competition was steep—the retail store I worked in had the number one and number two sales reps in the division. I was the new guy, and my attitude was gratitude to God that I only needed one job, not three, to pay my bills. Plus, I was driven to prove to the sales manager who took a chance on me that her decision was the right one.

If I could beat my teammates in the store, I knew I had a shot at winning this entire contest! With a firm referral base and an excellent knowledge base of our products and services, Derrek, the number one sales guy on the team, was always at the top of the leaderboard. Jessica was quickly giving Derrek a run for his money. Like me, she was a newer team member and was as smart as she was beautiful. Working in a Navy town gave her one heck of an advantage. Everyone else seemed to be just going through the motions and not motivated to win much more than a paycheck every two weeks.

So I observed Derrick and Jessica to see if I was missing anything. What I quickly learned was Derrick was the king of pre-qualifying his customers. Our store faced the parking lot with huge windows, so we could see customers long before they entered the store. I noticed that Derrick had a habit of needing something from the back when customers with less than gleeful faces and bills in hand would approach the store. I swear he had a sixth sense; without even looking up, he could feel them approaching and would just disappear.

Jessica, on the other hand, was just as hungry as me—we both hated losing at anything. We would even race each other to be first at staff meetings. Our boss loved it. Over the years, we would go out of our way to one-up each other, even on gifts to our boss! She was the perfect nemesis and constantly drove me to do better. Thank you, Jessica!

So I reviewed the contest rules and then worked out my plan. With no cap on new sales, new accessory sales, or payments, it was simple. Since I could not compete with Derrick's robust referral network or Jessica attracting all the sailors in a 100-mile radius, my plan was simple: *grind*! I would get into the office early to get all admin and other tasks completed long before my shift started. As a rule, it was frowned upon to be on the sales floor before your shift, but no one had an issue if you took problems or payments. So every time I was on the floor early, I would let the sales team know, "I'm here a little early, but I'm only taking payments or problems." Before my selling time even started, I would take 10–15 payments on average—15 points!

When Derrick conveniently needed something from the back, I would grab a few more points, upsell, and ask for referrals. When Jessica had literally lines of sailors waiting for her, I would pick off more points. More times than I could count, I would look over and see her glaring at me as her customer would be dragging out his sale to flirt with her. I would smile and just keep grabbing more points. Once in a while, I would save her and come over to assist her since she had others waiting. She was very thankful.

This went on day in and day out for weeks. The more payments and problems I solved, the more sales started to gather. Referrals began pouring in, and my ability to upsell new customers grew, as well as every payment and problem upsell. I became a master of the systems and could take payments, solve problems, and sell new products simultaneously. I never had a line, I greeted every customer, and I treated every customer as I wanted to be treated, even selling products for my co-workers when they were off or already busy.

When the first contest update was released, everyone but me was shocked that I was the leader of not only the store but the region, by a big margin. My peers quickly requested meetings with the manager, and once they did a deep dive, the difference was the payments. I took in 10–20 times the payments of my peers! I was a close third in new sales overall, but it was the payments that drove me to the top.

Everyone assumed it must be easy to just take more payments. It was, but once they started taking more payments, they would see potential sales walk in, and they would lose those. Once they had a few payments with problems, they quickly reverted to their old ways. But not me; the grind was on! I knew becoming number one was easy; keeping the spot was the hard part. I assumed everyone else in the region knew my secret and was taking advantage of this. I put my head down and continued with my daily grind. When I finally looked up, I was drinking a daiquiri on the beach in the Caribbean!

Twenty years later, as I speak with sales reps across the country, I'm always asked the same two questions: 1) "How have you succeeded at sales?" and 2) "How are the top sales reps selling so much more than the rest of their peers?" The answer is always the same, and the less-than-successful reps look surprised. It is a regimented routine of daily tasks that are repeated, repeated, repeated, and yes, you guessed it, repeated. Day in and day out, they execute a task-ordinated routine that has been fine-tuned over time. They do this with a positive mental attitude and are truly leveraging *atticution*. It's nothing fancy and is, at times, very mundane, but they get the importance of it. They love the process, they love the routine, and they know it yields the results they and their company need.

Executing on this level every day is what separates the average from the extraordinary. There are examples of those who are naturally talented and must work very little on their craft, but they are rare and often never reach their full potential. For the rest of us, the grind is the great equalizer and can take us anywhere we want to go. I have heard it said that discipline, or the grind, leads to freedom. It's true, and the more discipline you have, the more freedom you can have.

Attitude Check

- How do you feel when you have to do the same task day in and day out?

- Do you love or already like the grind?

- What do you need to change about your attitude to at least like the grind?

Execution Exercise

- Professional: Write down your daily tasks Monday – Friday. Hour by hour, what are you doing? Does it deliver the results you desire? What should you be doing?

- Personal: Write down how you spend your time. Are you on social media all night, experiencing FOMO (fear of missing out) and missing out on what is in front of you?

- Build your grind plan!

7

Do Your Job

Individuals win games. Teams win championships.

It was the fourth quarter of the first game of the season, and the local peewee football team was driving down the field for the game-winning score. The center hiked the ball, the offensive line held back the oncoming rush, and the quarterback handed the ball off to the lightning-fast running back who cut outside and was about to make his turn upfield. The wide receiver, my youngest son, who was the shortest, lightest player on the team, was doing what his coaches have worked on with him for weeks—he had his hands up and was blocking his much larger, much heavier opponent. A quick block, just enough to free the running back, and he was off! Forty-plus yards later, he scored the winning touchdown, and the overzealous crowd cheered for the star running back!

I, on the other hand, screamed at the top of my lungs, "Awesome job, buddy! That was the block of the day!" What the coaches and I knew is that without the line blocking rushers, the quarterback delivering a good handoff, the receivers on the other side of the field running their routes, and the under-sized receiver (my youngest son) doing his job, the star running back would be at the bottom of a pile of opponents.

As we walked to the car with their first official football game completed, my youngest looked at me with a puzzled look on his face. "What do you mean that without me we would not have won the game?" He had not put together that, as with any good team, everyone had to do their job and do it well to advance the ball.

I learned this lesson early in life with team sports and further refined and reshaped this skill in my Navy career. In the Navy, there are real consequences of someone not doing his or her job. Each role inside the company has a serious impact up and down the chain of command. A sales rep who does not do the job of setting the right expectation for post-sale next steps can cause more work for the support teams. The customer service representative who does not take the time to listen to the new customer's concerns and seek to understand the overall or real concern can send the customer up the chain of command, costing the company serious time, money, and energy, or worse, a customer.

Attitude Check

- What is your role in this overall big picture?

- What happens when your job is not done well?

- What happens when it is done well?

- How do you feel after completing a task that impacts the overall picture?

Execution Exercise

- List ten aspects of the business that your role impacts.

    o List the outcomes of poor execution.

o List the outcomes of excellent execution.

o What can you do differently to execute better?

8

Balance

The key is not to prioritize what's on your schedule, but to schedule your priorities.

—Steven Covey

The parking lot was empty as I pulled up to the dimly lit van. I could make out the shaggy-haired man donning his wetsuit. With a huge grin, my surf coach, Barry, greeted me. "Dude! Perfect conditions." This guy was the definition of a surf coach, from his warm surfer soul to his almost always tan face. We planned our lesson early that Saturday to beat the rush and catch the tide at the best time for a newbie surfer like me.

We zipped up our wetsuits, grabbed our freshly waxed boards, and headed down the steps to the water. Predawn Santa Cruz was pitch black as we prepared to paddle out to open water, so I fully engaged my mind in the process. We paddled out to what only Barry could see as the perfect spot. Sitting atop our boards, we chatted about how to read the water even with little to no light, what the conditions were today, what that meant to our lesson, how the board I was using was smaller than last time, what time the tide was coming in, and where we needed to be by when. It was so much information I almost forgot I was floating around in Monterey Bay in total darkness in an area known to have large sharks!

"Okay, start paddling!"

I turned my board toward the shore and started paddling. Barry would stop mid-sentence to get me ready for the wave.

"A little faster and a little more right," I heard over my shoulder. I could feel the energy of the wave under me and began to pop up. The wave was small but perfect for me and my current skill level. I kept my eye toward the shore and my body steady as the wave carried me further and further. As the wave lost its energy, I slid back into the water. I was pumped up from riding the first wave, and the sun had not even risen yet.

As I paddled back out, the sun was starting to rise—a perfect start to a relaxing day. For the next three hours, I tried to catch, and sometimes caught, a wave, but I never once thought about the stressful work week I'd just had or the even more stressful week ahead. All I thought about was catching the next wave, when to paddle faster, what the right swell in the water was, and whatever else I could learn from the ultimate waterman.

We've all heard that you should work hard and play hard, but we must relax even harder. Working hard is a given. In today's professional world, you have to work hard just to maintain the status quo. Most books will also add work smarter not harder, but I believe that you have to relax harder so you can both work harder and work smarter. Much is written about the need to balance our lives on the seasons and cycles of the earth from winter to summer and back again, the daily rhythm of our own bodies, and how that is thrown off track when we get too much or too little sleep. All of that is true; we must keep this balance in mind.

Today, more than ever, we also need to prioritize relaxing and downtime. The harder or more you work, the more information and content is being fed into your brain. We live in a world where we must have a smartphone, laptop, tablet, smartwatch, and 24-hour access to Wi-Fi. We are connected and getting more connected each day with no focus on our balance and the need to not just disconnect but fully disconnect. I have picked up two hobbies that help me disconnect and clear my mind—surfing and scuba diving. Funny how you have to literally submerge your body ten feet below the water to be fully disconnected! But I'm sure someone in some start-up in Silicon Valley is developing underwater Wi-Fi as you read this.

Relax hard. What does that mean? It means plan your downtime as you would your work time, but challenge yourself to find new hobbies or challenges that work your brain so that you have to give that task 100% of your attention. Really push yourself to try something new. This does not have to be some adrenaline-filled new hobby or even something out of your comfort zone (at first, but that should change); it just needs to be something new to consume your mind for an extended time.

Everyone I have met has something they have always wanted to try. "Someday" is their answer. Dads and Moms, you could pick up a joystick and play a video game with your kids. Maybe it's something simple like family dinner night, except you make something really different and engage the whole family. Play board games, put together a jigsaw puzzle, try yoga, take a fly fishing class—you are only limited by your imagination.

Attitude Check

- Do you have downtime? Do you plan your downtime?

- How do you think about your time?

  - Do you think it's a waste of time? How many great ideas have come to you when you were doing something else?

- What new skill or hobby have you wanted to do but couldn't find the time for or were too scared to try?

  - Your only regrets will be the chances you don't take.

Execution Exercise

- Make a list of the times you've planned your personal downtime.

- Brainstorm ideas and possible hobbies that could engage 100% of your mind for an extended time.

- Do it! Stop making excuses such as not having time, not wanting to do something for just you, being too old, or being too young. *Just do it!*

  o You must do things for yourself. If you don't take care of yourself physically and mentally, *you cannot take care of those around you!*

  o This may come off as selfish, but the question still remains—if you're sick, who will be able to take care of those around you?

Conclusion

You do not get paid for the hour. You get paid for the value you bring to the hour.

—Jim Rohn

Invest in yourself more than your job. I often get funny looks when I say this in a work setting. Once I ask a few follow-up questions, the point is made. First, if you focus on improving your skill set and value, who else benefits? Yup, the company you work for! Second, once you have new skills and increased value, who else sees the positive impact? That's right. The company you work for! Third, if the company supports and even encourages you to increase your value and skill set, how loyal would you be to that company? Very loyal.

When I move on to asking what other value this brings, people rattle off a dozen or so other benefits about home life, health, energy, and so on, which all leads back to the main point: invest in yourself first! This book is one way and one step to investing in yourself. You have to take action, whether through this book or something else that continues to push you out of your comfort zone, to create an environment that not only enables you to grow but also enriches those around you. Whether a big leap or small steps toward a better you, taking action starts with the right attitude and is reached with atticution.

Workbook

Chapter 1: Motivation Is Just an Alarm Clock

Attitude Check

- When was the last time you felt motivated?

- What actions did you take or not take to act in that moment?

- What can you use as a daily alarm clock to get you motivated?

Execution Exercise

List your top three motivation sources, such as family, friends, videos, etc.

1. _____

2. _____

3. _____

List two or more people who can help you stay motivated.

1. _____

2. _____

3. _____

4. _____

Find an event with a defined date to focus on (e.g., 5k fun run, half marathon, vacation, wedding, reunion, etc.), anything that can help push you toward your goal. *And* sign up today to do it! Take action *now!* Seriously—stop, find it, and sign up!

_____

_____

_____

_____

_____

_____

_____

Chapter 2: Accountability Partners: Build Your Tribe

Attitude Check

- Think of who you trust and can ask for help in your circle of influence (professional and personal).

- In what areas of your life would you like some accountability?

- When could you meet, and how often?

Execution Exercise

Make a list of five people you trust and value who can keep you accountable.

1. _____

2. _____

3. _____

4. _____

5. _____

Schedule a call with your list and explain your *why* and how you value them. Then tell them you would appreciate their help.

_____

_____

_____

_____

_____

_____

_____

_____

Schedule time away from the normal interaction with these five people, communicate your goals, and let them know how they can help you (and vice versa).

Chapter 3: Challenge Yourself

Attitude Check

- What new skill or challenge have you completed in the last 90 days?

- What new books have you read or classes have you taken in the last year?

- What is your limiting factor for why you are not challenging yourself?

Execution Exercise

Go write your goals down! Now. Go big or go home! Your goals need to be a stretch, not a layup.

Communicate them with friends and family. I have found that telling my boys is the ultimate accountably.

_____

_____

_____

_____

ATTICUTION

_____

_____

_____

_____

Chapter 4: Write It Down: Goals, Action Items, Commitments

Attitude Check

- What is your attitude toward goals?

- What is stopping you from writing your goals down?

Execution Exercise

What are your top five goals in these categories? Mark them as long-term (L), medium-term (M), or short-term (S) goals.

Top 5 Goals	Date	L/M/S
Professional:		
1.		
2.		
3.		
4.		
5.		

Health (Fitness, Emotional, Spiritual, and Social):		
1.		
2.		
3.		
4.		
5.		
Financial:		
1.		
2.		
3.		
4.		
5.		
Personal Development:		
1.		
2.		
3.		
4.		
5.		

Review these goals with your accountability partner or tribe, a trusted friend, a co-worker, or someone else. Schedule this conversation now.

_____

_____

_____

_____

_____

_____

_____

_____

If you are a leader, schedule time with our team and build your top five team goals together.

1. _____

2. _____

3. _____

4. _____

5. _____

If you're not a leader yet, this will go a long way with your leadership since they might not have had the chance to do this themselves. *Side note:* setting team goals as a single unit builds unity and trust.

Additionally, communicate with as many people as possible; this will help hold you accountable.

Chapter 5: SMAART Goals

Attitude Check

- When was the last time you were able to reach a goal you set?

- What goals would bring you the most joy if you reached them in the next 12-24 months?

- What are the major obstacles that you would face in reaching those goals?

Execution Exercise

Write down at least 20 goals leveraging the SMAART system (use the following worksheet).

SMAART Work Sheet

Goal	Term	Accountability	Success
1.			
2.			
3.			
4.			

5.			
6.			
7.			
8.			
9.			
10.			
11.			
12.			
13.			
14.			
15.			
16.			
17.			
18.			
19.			
20.			

Chapter 6: Do What Winners Do — Grind

Attitude Check

- How do you feel when you have to do the same task day in and day out?

- Do you love or already like the process?

- What do you need to change about your attitude to at least like the process?

Execution Exercise

Professional: Write down your daily tasks Monday – Friday. Hour by hour, what are you doing? Does it deliver the results you desire? What should you be doing?

Monday:

AM:_____

PM: _____

Tuesday

AM:_____

PM:_____

Wednesday

AM:_____

PM:_____

Thursday

AM:_____

PM:_____

Friday

AM:_____

PM:_____

Saturday

AM:_____

PM:_____

Sunday

AM:_____

PM:_____

Date	What am I doing?	What should I be doing?

Personal: Write down how you spend your time. Are you on Social media all night experiencing FOMO (fear of missing out) and missing out on what is in front of you?

- Facebook: _____

- LinkedIn: _____

- Instagram: _____

- TV/Netflix: _____

- YouTube: _____

Chapter 7: Do Your Job

Attitude Check

- What is your role in this overall big picture?

- What happens when your job is not done well?

- What happens when it is done well?

- How do you feel after completing a task that impacts the overall picture?

Execution Exercise

List ten aspects of the business your role impacts.

1. _____

2. _____

3. _____

4. _____

5. _____

6. _____

7. _____

8. _____

9. _____

10. _____

List the outcomes of poor execution.

1. _____

2. _____

3. _____

4. _____

5. _____

6. _____

7. _____

8. _____

9. _____

10. _____

List the outcomes of good execution.

1. _____

2. _____

3. _____

4. _____

5. _____

6. _____

7. _____

8. _____

9. _____

10. _____

What can you do differently to execute better?

1. _____

2. _____

3. _____

4. _____

5. _____

6. _____

7. _____

8. _____

9. _____

10. _____

Chapter 8: Balance

Attitude Check

- Do you have downtime? Do you plan your downtime?

- How do you think about your time?

  - Do you think it's a waste of time? How many great ideas have come to you when you were doing something else)?

- What new skill or hobby have you wanted to do but couldn't find the time for or were too scared to try?

  - Your only regrets will be the chances you don't take.

Execution Exercise

Make a list of the times you've planned your personal downtime.

1. _____

2. _____

3. _____

4. _____

Brainstorm ideas and possible hobbies that could engage 100% of your mind for an extended time.

_____

_____

_____

_____

_____

_____

_____

_____

Do it! Stop making excuses such as not having time, not wanting to do something for just you, being too old, or being too young. *Just do it!*

- You must do things for yourself. If you do not take care of yourself physically and mentally, *you cannot take care of those around you!*

- This may come off as selfish, but the question remains—if you're sick, who will be able to take care of those around you?

_____

_____

_____

_____

_____

_____

_____